Winnipeg

Walks

by
the Prairie Pathfinders

Text & Editing	Wendy Wilson Leone Banks
Photography	Sheila Spence Wendy Wilson
Research	Leone Banks Kathleen Leathers
Design & Maps	Wendy Wilson
Field Study	Leone Banks Wendy Wilson Kathleen Leathers
Project Development	Leone Banks Sheila Spence

Winnipeg Walks
Copyright ©1998 Prairie Pathfinders Inc.

Published by Prairie Pathfinders Inc.
PO Box 26074
Winnipeg, Manitoba, Canada R3C 4K9

Printed in Canada by City Press
Winnipeg, Manitoba

First Edition
ISNB 0-9683976-0-3

Canadian Cataloguing In Publication Data
Main entry under title:

Winnipeg walks

     ISBN 0-9683976-0-3

1. Walking--Manitoba--Winnipeg--Guidebooks.
2. Winnipeg (Man.)--Tours. I. Prairie Pathfinders (Association).

FC3396.18.W55 1998   917.127'4304   C98-920131-7
F1064.5.W7W55 1998

A grant from the Winnipeg Foundation, a contributor to the quality of life in our community since 1921, helped make this publication possible.

Cover Photograph: *Whittier Park looking west by Sheila Spence*

Introduction

Learning about Winnipeg and appreciating its different neighbourhoods, is best done on foot. If you really want to see the city you have to get out and walk around it - witness it firsthand.

This book describes thirty-three of the best walks in and around Winnipeg and tells something of the character and local history of different neighbourhoods as well as plants and animals that might be seen along the way. You'll discover the beauty of an abandoned rail line in Charleswood and the charm of worker cottages in Point Douglas. You'll find lots of surprises including a terrific system of linear parkways along our rivers and streams and you'll find that walking is an excellent way to have fun while you're keeping fit.

Winnipeg Walks is intended for anyone who can walk a trail, however slowly and for those who have never tried. We hope you will enjoy this book for sightseeing, history, nature walks, fitness, family adventure and just socializing.

Prairie Pathfinders are a non profit group organized with the goal of sharing knowledge of Manitoba's outstanding walking opportunities and promoting Winnipeg as a 'walkers city'. Through our Website, we'll share our latest discoveries and more in-depth information on many of our walks, as well as updates on trail conditions. Our long-term goal is a comprehensive documentation of recreational walking paths in our province.

Visit our Website:

www.prairiepathfinders.mb.ca

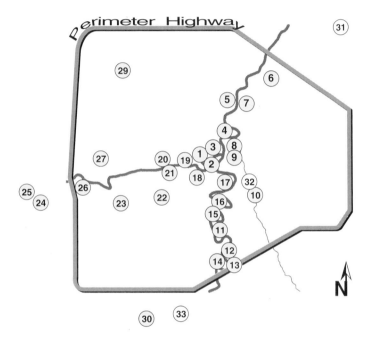

In most instances, our maps make clear where the walks are located and the best route to their starting points but we're recommending that you have a good city street map for reference.

NOTE:
Walks #31, #32 & #33 are winter walks.

Contents

1	Assiniboine Parkway	6
2	Osborne Village	8
3	Forks Circle	11
4	Point Douglas	14
5	Scotia Street	18
6	Bunn's Creek	22
7	Kildonan Drive	24
8	Old St Boniface	26
9	Central St Boniface	30
10	Niakwa Park	34
11	St Vital	35
12	Normand Park	37
13	Maple Grove	39
14	King's Park	41
15	Crescent Drive	44
16	Wildwood	46
17	Riverview	48
18	Crescentwood	50

19	Wolseley Wellington Cres	52
20	Bruce Park	56
21	Old Tuxedo	60
22	Assiniboine Forest	64
23	Harte Trail Charleswood	66
24	Harte Trail Headingly	68
25	Beaudry	70
26	Southboine	72
27	Sturgeon Creek Parkway	76
28	Living Prairie	80
29	Little Mountain Park	82
30	LaBarrier	84
31	Bird's Hill Park	86
32	Seine River Parkway	88
33	St Norbert LaSalle	90
	Manitoba Recreational Trail Association & Trans Canada Trail	93
	Guide to Public Transportation	94
	Selected Bibliography	95

Start	River path at east end of Cornish
Distance	5 km
Parking	Cornish Avenue

This is a classic urban walk with superb views from the Assiniboine Parkway. A quiet woodlands path takes you to the well landscaped River Walk. Then after crossing the Midtown bridge, return down River Avenue & Roslyn Rd; and end with a tour of majestic Armstrong Point.

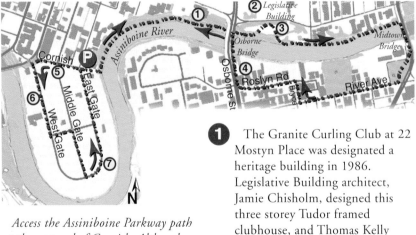

Access the Assiniboine Parkway path at the east end of Cornish. Although this parkway suffers severe erosion each spring, it is heavily used by the locals.

1   The Granite Curling Club at 22 Mostyn Place was designated a heritage building in 1986. Legislative Building architect, Jamie Chisholm, designed this three storey Tudor framed clubhouse, and Thomas Kelly built it in 1909.

2   The Legislative Building. Constructed of native tyndall

stone quarried east of Selkirk, this is an example of neoclassical architecture on a grand scale. The magnificent Golden Boy that tops the dome is 16 feet from toe to torch and was cast in France by Charles Gardet.

3 This 16 foot statue was erected by the Manitoba Metis Foundation to commemorate Louis Riel. Riel was a controversial figure whose contribution to Canadian history was much disputed until he was accorded status as the founding father of Manitoba in 1992.

4 When built in 1909, the Roslyn represented the height of elegant apartment living in Winnipeg.

5 The tyndall stone gates of Armstrong Point are a city landmark. They mark entrance to one of the city's oldest neighbourhoods with buildings rich in historic and architectural significance. Armstrong Point's location began to attract the attention of Winnipeg's economic elite by the late 1880's and early 1900's when three streets with large lots were laid out down the length of the peninsula.

6 55 West Gate was built for Charles Gordon a.k.a. Ralph Connor in 1914. Connor became wealthy at the turn of the century writing popular novels such as "Glengarry School Days" and "The Sky Pilot". The house has been the home of the University Women's Club since 1933.

7 Eden House at 147 East Gate was built in 1882 and is the oldest house in the neighbourhood. In earlier days there was a tennis court on the seven acres behind the

house which the neighbours called the Bird Cage Club. The property was later divided into three lots and sold.

Start	Legislative Buildings on Broadway Ave
Distance	6.5 km

This is a sidewalk route that loops through the heart of the city.

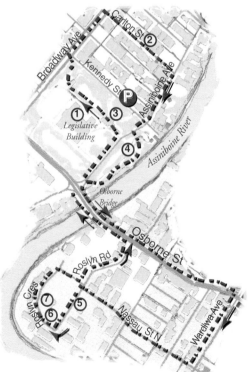

1 Our Legislative Building displays a wealth of ornamental detail and its grand interior spaces are well worth a tour.

2 Dalnavert is an example of Queen Anne Revival architecture and is among the last of the many old mansions that once stood in this part of the city. Most have been demolished to make room for office buildings, parking and apartment blocks. It was built in 1895 by the only son of Canada's first Prime

Minister - Hugh John Macdonald. The name "Dalnavert" commemorates both his father's home in Toronto and his maternal grandmother's birthplace in Scotland.

As was the fate of other big houses in the Broadway area, Dalnavert was a rooming house from 1929-1969 when the Manitoba Historical Society purchased the house and began restoration

3 Government House, on the southeast grounds of the Legislative Building, is a stylish piece of architecture with its wrought iron and mansard roof. It was built in 1883 and is the

Queen's official residence in Manitoba and home of our Lieutenant Governor.

4 The demonstration gardens on the Legislative grounds are a great place for gardening enthusiasts to check out different species of plants. Begun in 1997, the head gardener for the province has set up a series of beds on the riverbank for flowers, vegetables, and shrubs. There is also an arboretum with the different trees tagged for identification.

Cross Osborne Bridge into the most densely populated neighbourhood in western Canada.

The five blocks of Osborne Street that make up the heart of 'the village' have a vibrancy and a sense of community that are hard to define or understand. A somewhat Bohemian quality pervades this popular commercial and residential area. Perhaps it's left over from the 60's when this was headquarters for hippie culture.

With the building of the Osborne bridge in 1882 and Winnipeg's first

gardener's cottage. Built in 1910, it was relocated ten years later to its present site by the front entry gates. During the Depression, it was renovated and expanded, reusing materials such as oak panelling and the Tudor mantel from the demolished mansion. In 1935, the widowed Lady Nanton made this her residence.

7 Nanton House Stables - 61 Roslyn Cres.

The original plan of these Tudor style stables was a U shape building surrounding an open carriage court The buildings were renovated for residential use in 1940, but retained many distinctive elements such as the wooden cupola.

electrified streetcar line in the decade following, Fort Rouge experienced a boom. Many residents living on Corydon and Gertrude in the early 1880's were engaged in the building trades or the burgeoning railway industry with its major Fort Rouge yards to the south. In the areas closer to the Assiniboine River, lots were larger and the grandest residential structures were found near the bridge.

5 218 Roslyn Cres

Passers-by are drawn to the elegant plaster ornamentation of Moss House. With its formal symmetry and handsome proportions, it is surprising to learn that four different architects over a period of 15 years had a hand in its design.

Roslyn Crescent was the site of the great Augustus Nanton estate - one of the grandest houses in Winnipeg. Although the main house was demolished in 1935, the entrance gates, stables and gatehouse remain.

6 "The Cottage" - 229 Roslyn Rd

The Nanton Estate Gatehouse may have originally been a

Start The Forks
Distance 2.8 km

The river-front walkways of this circle route take you through the historic heart of Winnipeg. The paths are well lit at night and aside from spring flood water, good walking winter and summer. As well, the Forks is a "destination walk". It's a great place to walk to restaurants or shopping or the many public events held at this site.

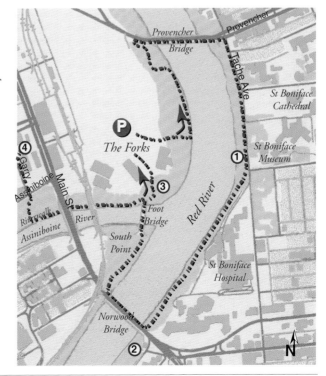

and Assiniboine rivers is once again a vibrant and popular meeting place.

 In 1844, four Grey Nuns from Montreal landed on these banks. It had been a long and difficult journey - 59 days by canoe. They had come to teach, but soon realized they were far more needed as nurses. They set up an infirmary and over the next 10 years made thousands of calls to the tents and shanties, ministering to the sick. In 1871, the Grey Nuns founded St. Boniface General Hospital - now one of the largest and most respected research and teaching health centres in western Canada.

From the Forks Market, walk north and cross the Provencher Bridge; turn right onto Tache Ave and proceed south, passing St. Boniface Cathedral and Museum; then take the asphalt path behind St. Boniface Hospital to the Norwood Bridge; cross and return to the Forks along the 'South Point' pathway.

The importance of this famous junction of the Red and Assiniboine rivers can be traced back 5000 years when it served as an assembly point for the aboriginal people. It was a critical link in the western fur trade and European settlement, and later, a major debarkation point for immigrants to western Canada. It is sad this place of such importance throughout history lay neglected and deserted for more than half a century. But its value to us has finally come full circle. With The Forks development, the junction of the Red

2 *side trip* - Pass under the Norwood Bridge and up to Lyndale Drive, then through one of the more popular residential areas

of the city - Norwood Flats. This neighbourhood has a secluded feel, despite being so close to downtown. Much of the neighbourhood is similar to the Wildwood Park development in that there are no front streets.

3 **Oodena - The Celebration Circle** is one of the most interesting sites at The Forks. "Oodena" is an Ojibway word meaning "heart of the community". This outdoor sanctuary with its grassy slopes and sandstone pillars, focuses our attention on the natural cycle of the stars, sun and moon. At night, searchlights from within the pillars create teepees in the sky to further direct our attention upwards.

4 *side trip - Upper Fort Garry -* Take the Assiniboine River Walk west under the Main St Bridge to Bonnycastle Park where a wide set of concrete steps lead up to Assiniboine Ave. Cross the street and take the east sidewalk of Garry St to Upper Fort Garry.

This small park contains Fort Garry Gate, all that remains of the famous fort. Upper Fort Garry was the commercial and administrative centre of the prairies from the 1830s to the 1880s. Plaques positioned around the park outline the history of the fort and the beginnings of the City of Winnipeg.

Start	The Forks
Distance	8 km

This walk through Winnipeg's oldest neighbourhood is full of historic and architectural interest, as well as a few surprises. Beginning at the Forks, it offers sweeping riverscapes of old St. Boniface while wending through Juba Park and on past the Alexander Docks.

1 To descend to the River Walk, find the "Wall of Time", which gives an account of events at the Forks from prehistory to the fur trade era.

2 A wooden dyke leads to Stephen Juba Park - named for one of Winnipeg's more colourful mayors. Bordered by mighty elms and cottonwoods, this park is a welcome

splash of green in the downtown area, and stretches from the Provencher Bridge to May Street.

A walkway leads around the Harbour Master headquarters at the end of James Avenue. This is the site referred to when river water levels are recorded in Winnipeg.

3 The 600 foot Alexander Dock is the last remnant of commercial shipping on the Red. From 1859-

1876, Point Douglas was the heart of river commerce. Steamboats brought settlers, supplies and construction materials from the U.S., and floating department stores on flatbeds would arrive to deal directly with residents.

4 Note the Scots monument erected by the St. Andrews Society.

It honours the 400 Selkirk Settlers who arrived between 1812 and 1814 to begin a farming community. Nearby posts outline the entrance to Fort Douglas. Fields to the west, named Colony Gardens by the early settlers, were planted with vegetables and feed grain by the Hudson's Bay Co. to sustain the settlers when they first arrived.

A newly landscaped gravel path, bordered by a heavy growth of prairie sage and cotton burdock, leads to Annabella Street. This is part of a recreational path from

The Forks to Kildonan Park which is the first designated link of the Trans Canada Trail in Manitoba.

At the foot of Curtis Street is a lovely old frame house with a giant cottonwood in the yard. Most of the

rebellion.

In the early part of this century, Point Douglas was distinctly rural. Everyone kept a cow and chickens. You may eye a garage or outer building with an odd appearance, and that will no doubt be because it started out as a horse barn.

At the north end of Stephens St. stands a giant cottonwood which may be 180-200 years old and is the largest tree in downtown Winnipeg. It was growing on the banks of the Red River when

homes here are a pleasant surprise, and this block is affectionately called "Artland", as many residents are associated with the Arts.

Annabella St. takes you across to the north side of Point Douglas. In the early part of the century, this street was famous for bootleg liquor and over 50 brothels.

The first and only Selkirk settlers to farm the point were Kate and Alexander Sutherland. They built their house where Sutherland Avenue now ends, but the great flood of 1852 carried their log cabin all the way across the river to St. Boniface. Rather than build anew, they purchased land there and became neighbours of the Lagimodieres and the Riels. Perhaps as a result, their only child John came to speak French and Cree and later was an important peacemaker between the Metis and the settlers during the 1869-70 Red River

the Selkirk Settlers arrived.

Point Douglas was to become Winnipeg's first elite neighbourhood. Dry goods agent E.L. Barber's house, built in 1867, is the oldest house still standing in the city. The Ashdown home, which used to stand at 109 Euclid, was an example of the mansions built by later arrivals in the neighbourhood and were in marked contrast to the simple Barber house. In 1877

J.H. Ashdown built a substantial three storey brick house with furnace and indoor plumbing. It was complete with circular driveway, flower beds and furniture imported from Minnesota.

As you look around from Joe Zuken Heritage Park you have a real sense of the age of the neighbourhood. Ross House, Winnipeg's first post office, is a prime example of Red River construction and was made almost entirely of hand carved log timber.

The first train steamed over the Louise bridge and west along the length of Point Douglas in July 1881. The arrival of that first train marked a watershed for the neighbourhood. It meant railway yards, industry, noise, smell and smoke. The genteel tranquillity that had lured Winnipeg's upper crust soon vanished. Mansions and lots were subdivided and small working class houses were crowded in beside faded mansions.

Today Point Douglas has a diverse population. Many families have lived here for 40-50 years. Recently there has been a renewed interest in the area, and when the new recreational trail around the point is completed the appeal of this unique neighbourhood will be enhanced.

6 *side trip* - *On the back lane, landscaped with evergreen and flowering shrubs and running between Market and Bannatyne Streets, enter the Exchange district - a 20 block area of fine turn-of-the-century commercial buildings and warehouses. Some have been restored for housing, restaurants and a variety of businesses. Most merchants will have a copy of the historic walking tour of this area.*

Start	Kildonan Park
Distance	4.5 km one way
Parking	Parking lot at Pavillion

This is a walk straight through the early history of our city. Beginning in carefully manicured Kildonan Park, our route takes us down Scotia St, south towards the onion domes of Holy Trinity Cathedral. The tour ends at historic St. John's Cathedral Cemetery and Winnipeg's oldest park.

1 One of the most striking things about this park is the lovely creek with its footbridges and rolling terrain. The gravel paths and roadway circling the English Landscape design of this park are popular with walkers year round. Other features such as the outdoor theatre,

swimming pool, brilliant formal flower gardens and massive trees make this a jewel in Winnipeg's park system.

West Kildonan was the first agricultural settlement in western Canada. Between 1812 and 1814, sixty families were brought over from Scotland by Lord Selkirk.

They settled on this side of the river because it was free of heavy timber having been burned over some years earlier. This saved them the back breaking labour of clearing the land before breaking it and seeding their crops. The farms were long narrow lots having river frontage of 330 - 660 ft, and running two miles back from the river with another two mile 'hay privilege' beyond. The river frontage varied in accordance with the number of children in the family, with 66 additional feet given for each child.

Scotia Street was named for Old Scotia, Scotland, home of many of these settlers. It was originally a walking path that connected their rough log dwellings with a trading post in Point Douglas.

Seven Oaks House at 115 Rupertsland takes its name from a nearby creek where seven oaks once stood, also marking the site of the battle of that name. It was built in the 1850's by John Inkster, a Hudson's Bay man born in the Orkney Isles in 1799. He arrived in the settlement in 1824 and married Mary Sinclair (daughter of a Hudson's Bay Factor and a Cree mother). Mary was 'good with figures' and managed their store while John handled their other interests. John built this nine room house after establishing himself here as a prosperous farmer, free trader and merchant. He did part of the building himself, including the stone foundation which withstood the disastrous flood of 1852 when most other buildings in the area were washed away. It was constructed of oak logs which were floated down

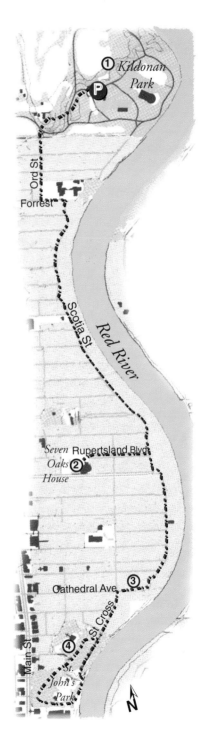

the Assiniboine & Red from Baie St. Paul (near Portage La Prairie). Shingles were handmade of cedar and glass; paint, putty, door locks, hinges, and nails were all brought out from England.

One 2nd floor bedroom belonged to Captain Colin Sinclair, who was Mary Inkster's brother. He settled here after more than 60 years at sea and refused to use a bed. He continued to sleep in his beloved hammock until he died in 1901. Today the hammock still hangs from its original hooks.

3 An historic tree with an arresting appearance stands at 57 Cathedral. The story goes that in 1851 it was used as a pulpit by John Black, our first Presbyterian minister, before he had a church. It is a Manitoba maple, usually upright and bushy, but it grew too close to a log cabin (long vanished) and its branches twisted to find the sun.

4 The graveyard around St. John's Cathedral is older than the church, and was used as early as 1812 by Selkirk Settlers. By the south east corner of the Cathedral an unusual piece of history is recorded on a pink granite monument. The inscription reads "Sacred to the memory of my mother, Margaret Sinclair. This last

token of love and affection is erected by her wandering boy Colin", the same Capt. Sinclair who slept in a hammock in Seven Oaks House. He was 81 when he had this inscribed, and had at last returned to his birthplace, seventy two years after he had left. In 1825 as a boy of nine, while visiting on a ship docked at Fort Prince of Wales, he fell asleep, and the Ship's Captain sailed away taking Colin to Scotland to be educated (as his dead father had

wished). This was done without Colin's mother's knowledge or consent, and she never saw him again. From Scotland Colin set out for a life at sea. But his attachment to his dead mother, to whom he hadn't said good-bye those many years before, brought him back for this final act of homage.

Bunn's Creek

Start	Henderson Hwy
Distance	2.6 km one way
Parking	Parking lot on west side of Henderson Hwy near Knowles

This gravel path along Bunn's Creek takes you from Henderson Hwy to McIvor Ave, through a beautifully natural linear parkway.

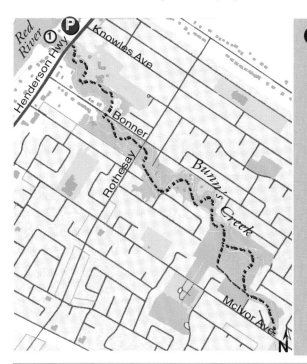

1 side trip

At the parking lot on the west side of Henderson Highway, a winding path takes you to forks of the Red River and Bunn's Creek and a view across the Red of McBeth Park and a stand of Plains cottonwood that are some of the oldest native trees still remaining in the city.

Hudson's Bay. He was schooled in Edinburgh and brought back to be the company surgeon at Moose Factory, in 1819. Over time he was employed to travel and give medical care to the entire area of settlement-from York Factory to the Red River Colony. He became a highly popular fellow recognized for extraordinary accomplishments. By 1835, Bunn was not only a physician, but also the coroner, clerk

Our path follows the creek as it meanders through 23 acres of park. Bunn's Creek Park provides the surrounding community of River East (a mix of large contemporary homes and older bungalows) with a country like atmosphere and is an ideal setting for a recreational foot path.

North Kildonan remained outside the area of intense urban settlement until the early 1970's. By this time the city's parks department was becoming interested in developing green spaces with wild or natural vegetation intact. Bunn's Creek as a 'natural' park is now a perfect model for the rest of the city.

The many lovely gardens that back onto the parkway are themselves worth the trip. One has been featured in a number of garden magazines.

The park and creek were named for the family of Dr. John Bunn, the Red River settlement's first Metis physician. Dr. Bunn was born in 1801 at a company post on

of the court, and sheriff. He gave much of his time to improving the health and social conditions of the colony and worked in the settlement until he died in 1881.

| **Start** | Fraser's Grove Park on Kildonan Dr |
| **Distance** | 2.2 km one way |

Walk through groves of elm and ash along the east bank of the Red River, through park that stretches away from the river like a large village green between Rossmere and Larchdale Crescents. On leaving the park walk down quiet and shady Kildonan Drive to the Bergen cut-off. Climb a path to walk atop the abandoned rail bed that leads to Henderson Hwy and a busy shopping and restaurant district.

abandoned rail bed ③

Irving Pl

Kildonan Park

Kildonan Drive

Henderson Hwy

Red River

Fraser's ① Grove Park

Rossmere ②

P

North Kildonan is part of the oldest settlement in our province. When Kildonan parish was first established by the Selkirk settlers in 1812, farmers occupied river lots on the western side of the river and used the well treed eastern side for fire wood. By 1820, when the west was filled up, people moved across and began to farm on former wood lots.

1 Fraser's Grove Park is named for a second generation Selkirk settler who generously allowed neighbours to picnic on his nicely wooded property. Over the years, Fraser's willingness to extend his hospitality beyond his circle of

friends made the area popular as a summer and winter fun spot.

Today it's possible to wander through Fraser Grove Park on a summer's night and listen to the music from Rainbow stage in Kildonan Park across the river.

2 A beautiful turn-of-the-century house at 135 Rossmere was originally a river lot farmhouse.

3 Water Mill Creek is now essentially filled-in, but at one time it wound its way across what is now Henderson Highway, Irving Place and Essar Ave. It once even boasted a water mill called Matheson Grist Mill.

Start	Whittier Park
Distance	5 km
Parking	Parking lot at end of Rue St Joseph

A walk through wilderness within sight of skyscrapers, this route mixes secluded paths on the banks of two rivers and rich history on the streets of Old St Boniface.

Walk along the Red through a strip of natural river bank woods to the mouth of the Seine River, then follow a narrow dirt path south under a railway bridge to a walking bridge over the Seine. Cross and turn left down a set of wooden steps to a landscaped river bank walkway. Return on city streets.

Whittier Park was a race track from the 1880's until 1925. The Park is named for poet John Greenleaf Whittier who paid homage to the St. Boniface Cathedral in the 1850's with the words, "The bells of the Roman Mission, That call from their turrets twain, To the boatman

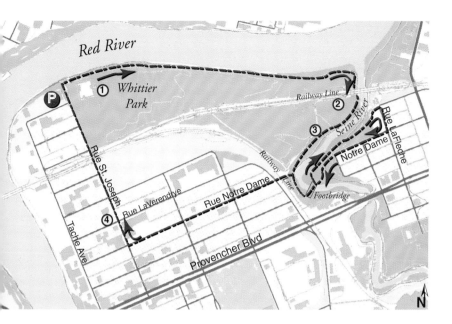

on the river - To the hunter on the plain."

Whittier Park comes alive each February during the Festival du Voyageur - the only time restored Fort Gibralter is open to the public. The original Fort was built in 1807 by the North West Fur Company. It was their halfway house on the 3000 mile fur route to Montreal.

The week long Festival brings Manitoba's French and fur trade heritage to the forefront.

An explorer in 1801 reported on an abundance of huge trees in this area - elm, basswood, poplar and oak so tall that their branches started 50 feet up the trunk. But by 1890 this area was completely denuded, as settlers had cut down all trees for building and firewood.

1 One elm survived. It is about 10 metres from the south turret of reconstructed Fort Gilbratar and

is believed to be over 260 years old. This heritage Whittier Park elm is 6 metres in diameter, 26 metres tall, and beautifully shaped.

The flood plain along the Red and Seine rivers is covered with

thick layers of alluvial soil. Scars on the tree trunks show where ice jams have gouged the trees during spring floods, and refuse stuck in the branches evidence the height of the 1997 flood.

3 Jean Baptiste and Marie Anne Lagimodiere, the first farmers in St. Boniface, built a log cabin here on the banks of the Seine in 1819. Lagimodiere is a legendary figure for his celebrated 5 month walk from Winnipeg to Montreal, carrying a plea for help from the Red River settlers to Lord Selkirk. As a result, he was awarded most of the land in this area including Whittier Park. Marie Anne is also the stuff of legends. She arrived here by canoe in 1806 and was the first white woman west of Lake Superior. Her first child, Julia, was born in 1807 in a wigwam pitched on the banks of the Pembina River south of Winnipeg. Julia was to become the mother of Louis Riel.

4 165 La Verendry St. is the oldest Winnipeg house still being used as a private residence. It was built in 1878 by Norman Kittson for his son as a wedding present. Norman Kittson was a businessman who introduced steamboat service between Winnipeg and St. Paul in 1860 and eventually made millions trading goods between Winnipeg and the U.S.

2 **side trip** *Informal paths crisscross the undeveloped parkland on both sides of the elevated rail line . This expanse of shrubs, wildflowers and the occasional knot of trees has an isolated feel. The Winnipeg skyline is always visible and any path heading west will return you to city streets.*

Start	Franco Manitoban Centre - 340 Provencher
Distance	6.5 km

This walk is through some of the city's most important cultural landmarks. The tour offers an interesting mix of architectural styles, as well as some fine views of the Seine River.

From the Franco-Manitoban Centre, proceed east along Provencher Blvd, crossing DesMeurons, until you reach the Seine River. On your right, find the newly constructed Seine River Interpretive Trail. This trail will take you south to Marion St. From that point, you will follow along sidewalks around the central area of Saint Boniface.

There has been a French presence in this area since Quebec fur traders arrived in the mid 1700's. Voyageurs working for the North West Co. settled in what is now St. Boniface with their native born wives. These French voyageurs fathered a new French speaking Catholic nation - the Metis.

After the clash between the Metis and the Selkirk Settlers in 1817, Lord Selkirk attempted to resolve the conflict by requesting the Roman

Catholic church to send missionaries from Quebec. He believed that the church would provide stability to the French-Catholic settlement. To encourage them to locate on the east side of the Red River, he granted the Catholic church a large plot of land there. In 1819 a small chapel was built. Most of the elements which shaped St. Boniface's character were in place by the early 1830s. The farm lots occupied by French Catholic settlers reached from the mouth of the Seine to the LaSalle River and beyond. Their community life centered upon the institutions and works of the St. Boniface mission - the centre and symbol of French Manitoba.

❶ La Vielle Gare - 630 Des Meurons
Now a fine French restaurant, this lovely railway station, built of bricks imported from Missouri,

served the people of southeast Manitoba for many years before becoming obsolete.

❸ King Edward School - 261 Youville
Built as a public school in 1915, it is a fine example of school architecture of that period. It is now a disignated historic building and home to The Springs Christian Academy.

❹ Enfield Crescent is a true crescent. At one time it skirted an oxbow of the Red River, and the slope of the ancient riverbank is still obvious. As the Red wanders across its plain, large loops evolve, similar to the one around Point Douglas. Oxbows are created as erosion cuts away at the base of the peninsula.

❷ *The Roy House - 375 Rue Deschambault*
The childhood home of Gabrielle Roy, one of Canada's most distinguished writers and author of fifteen books, including The Tin Flute, The Road Past Altamont and The Street of Riches, which describes her family's life on Rue Deschambault.

Eventually the river cuts through a new channel, and the old river bed becomes isolated, fills with silt, and becomes a marsh. The Enfield marsh appeared on maps prior to 1900.

 Precious Blood Church - 200 Kenny St
Designed by local architect Etienne Gaboury, the spiral form imitates the "teepee" of the prairies. Both exterior and interior are unique in terms of church architecture and well worth a tour.

 Locally named the "Kenny Street Elm", this historic elm is located on the west boulevard of Kenny Street near the junction of the rear lane of Kitson St. This elm figured prominently in the life of a well known young pioneer named Victor Mager. Mager had moved with his family from Lorraine, France, in 1859 to take residence near the present site of St. Boniface Hospital. In the early years, Mr. Mager regularly hunted wild game throughout the areas now referred to as Norwood and St. Vital. On one of his forays in 1889, he marked the tree with a cross, and it soon became a recognized landmark. The tree is still in good condition. and is about 70 feet high.

 Saint Boniface Museum - 494 Tache Ave
Originally a convent for the Grey Nuns, who arrived from Montreal in 1844, this national historic site built in 1846 is the oldest building in the city and the largest oak log construction in North America.

 Saint Boniface Cathedral - 190 Cathedral Ave
The Basilica built in 1908 was

destroyed by fire in 1968. The present structure, designed by Etienne Gaboury, incorporates the remaining Romanesque facade, arches, pillars and statue of Saint Boniface. In the cemetery you will find the final resting place of Louis Riel, recognised in 1992, as the founder of Manitoba.

 9 Archbishop's Palace - 141 Cathedral Ave
The western portion of the palace was built in 1864 and is one of the oldest stone structures still standing in western Canada. Note the elegant Mansard roof.

10 Saint Boniface College - 200 Cathedral Ave
The College's tradition of French education dates back to 1818. It now offers French study bachelor degrees in Arts, Science, Education and Translation.

11 Provencher School - 320 Cathedral Ave
The origin of the Provencher Institute for boys dates back to the arrival of Father Provencher. The location of the school changed three times before it finally resided in the present building, and it was not until 1968 that the school began to teach both boys and girls.

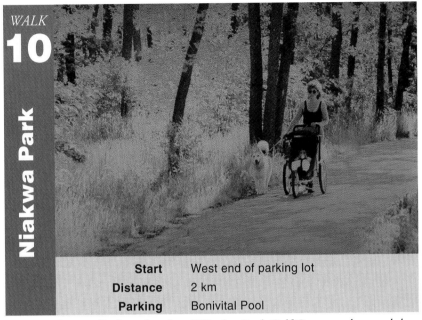

Start	West end of parking lot
Distance	2 km
Parking	Bonivital Pool

This is a short walk along the edge of Windsor Park Golf Course and around the circumference of the suburb of Niakwa Park.

From the parking lot at the Bonivital swimming pool, the route heads west following a chain link fence to the Seine River. Cross the foot bridge and turn left taking a dirt path that hugs the west bank of the river. This path is just a narrow ledge where the chain link fence butts up to the water. Continue on this trail until it joins an asphalt path running east-west. Turn left, crossing another foot bridge and into Papoose Park.

The cycle path along Archibald will return you to the Bonivital parking lot.

When Niakwa Park was designed after World War II, it was the first neighbourhood in Winnipeg to get away from the grid pattern and use the bay formation. The development grew rapidly, and for six years, between 1955 and 1961, a house was completed every day in Windsor Park and Niakwa Park.

Papoose Park was created at this time, when developers set aside six acres for green space.

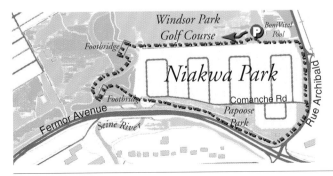

Start	Southwest corner of parking lot
Distance	2.4 km / side trip 1.6 km one way
Parking	Parking lot adjacent to duck pond

This walk takes you through the thickly wooded landscape of St. Vital Park and along the Red River to the site of a Metis farmhouse restored to the era of the early settlers.

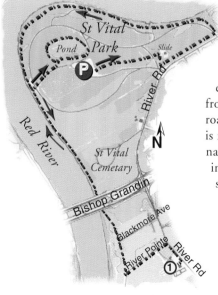

St Vital Park was originally designed for motorists. When the land was purchased by the city in 1929, the idea of using a park for a short automobile excursion drew popular response from the citizenry. The emphasis on roadways over walking paths however, is more than compensated by beautiful natural features of the park. Tucked into a bend of the Red River, are sections of thick woods, mixed with open meadows and outstanding viewpoints along the high river bank. Wide asphalt pathways border the centrepiece man-made lake and nearby rock garden.

Riel House

There are two routes to the Riel farm house, and the river bank route may require some agility, particularly when wet. The alternative route is down River Rd and across busy Bishop Grandin.

The river bank path continues south out of the park, past the cemetery ,and under Bishop Grandin. Cross Blackmore Ave to River Point Rd; then proceed east to River Rd.

This was the home of Louis Riel's family from 1880 to 1969. Riel House is now a National Historic Site. The national importance of Louis Riel is the raison d'etre of Riel House National Historic Park, but its interpretation focuses more specifically on the Riel family and Metis society during the 1860's. The Metis had pursued mixed farming in the parish of St. Vital since the 1830's, and Riel House displays the typical farm layout. The barn, chicken house, milk house, and other farm buildings were customarily located close to the

river bank for easy access to water and waste disposal. Small fenced and cultivated grain fields were located "at the back", or as in the case of the Riel Farm, in the area between the Red and Seine rivers. Beyond this, occupying the rest of the long narrow lot, was the larger hay field. Cattle were usually allowed to graze in unfenced areas around the barn and probably close to the residence . River Lot 51, occupied by the Riel family in the 1880's, was larger than a standard lot. It was twelve chains (792 ft.) in width and two miles in depth, for a total of 232 acres. The property also included a twenty four acre parcel at the Seine River or eastern boundary, where a grist mill was built around 1855.

Since the 1960's, urbanization had been creeping over this originally rural farming district. Since Riel House became an historic park in 1981, a housing development has been built to the west and much of the illusion of a river lot setting as it existed in the 1880's is gone.

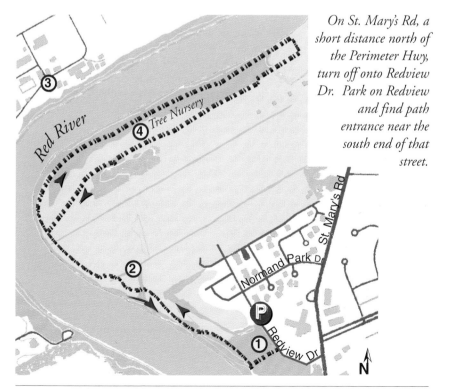

The first part of this walk is on a carefully landscaped pathway in a new residential development. The second half follows old trails along the river and through the old Henteleff nursery.

Start	Path entrance on Redview Dr
Distance	5 km
Parking	On Redview Dr

On St. Mary's Rd, a short distance north of the Perimeter Hwy, turn off onto Redview Dr. Park on Redview and find path entrance near the south end of that street.

1 This walk begins in an upscale housing development built in 1987 and designed in line with the city's new policy of preserving the river bank for recreation. The Residents' Association and Winnipeg Parks worked together to

build a walking path through existing native river forest vegetation with native grasses and flowers planted in the open areas of this 14 acre linear park.

2 A row of mature willows divide the residential portion of the walk from a dirt trail skirting fields of open meadow. Follow an informal path (that turns into a dirt road) running north and east along the river to the tree nursery.

3 Note the University of Manitoba skyline across the river. Watch for deer and fox in the fields.

4 This tree nursery, now operated by the city of Wpg, was once the Henteleff family market gardens. They cleared the land in the 1920's and ran their operation until the 60's when the city expropriated the land for a proposed 'Green Zone' around Winnipeg.

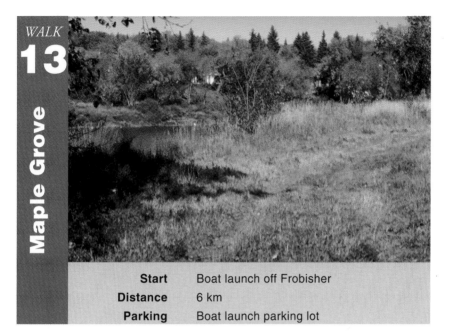

Maple Grove

Start	Boat launch off Frobisher
Distance	6 km
Parking	Boat launch parking lot

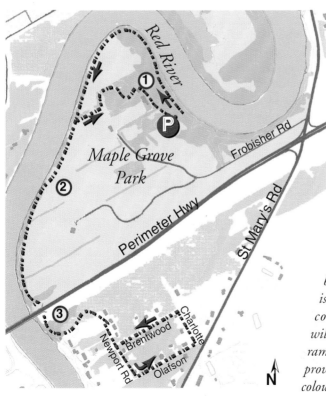

Skirting open fields and winding through mature native river forest, this informal pathway hugs the east bank of the Red River. Even though within sight of the Perimeter Hwy, one has the sense of being in some isolated part of the country. Rows of willow & maple and ramshackle buildings provide evidence of a colourful past.

Maple Grove 39

1 The path passes by a concrete block building, now used by Park employees, that was part of a thriving recreation area called Maple Grove Beach. During the forties, swimming, a dance hall, canoe rentals and baseball diamonds beckoned city dwellers to a day of fun 'in the country'. Having reached its peak of popularity as a picnic site

during World War II, the facilities were badly damaged in the 1952 flood, and then the beach was declared unsafe for swimming during the polio epidemic of '53.

2 For more than forty years (until the mid '60s), these open fields were home to five market garden operations that employed up to 50 people in a busy summer. They supplied vegetables to Safeway and other grocery stores in the city. In the early thirties, W.A. Taylor, a St. Boniface candy store owner, planted more than 10 acres of horse radish. It was processed on site and sold it under the label 'Poplar'.

The rows of trees that butt up to the riverbank at 1/8 mile intervals are evidence of land tenure based on the seigneurial system that was practiced by the early Metis settlers. From the early 1800's, long narrow river lots up to 3 km deep gave families access to water and transportation. Subsequently, the Canadian Government purchased the land from the Hudson's Bay Co and tried to impose the English land holding pattern on the settlers. This action was one major factor leading to the Metis Resistance of 1869.

The city, at various times, has made elaborate plans for the park's development - fishing piers, a swinging bridge across the river to King's Park, etc., but so far rugby and soccer fields have been the only developments. Nonetheless, the park is a popular all season walk, especially with dog owners, and it is hoped that a good portion of the area may be left in its natural state for all of us to enjoy.

3 *side trip* Continue on under the Perimeter Hwy through woods of scrub oak and Hawthorn to Newport Rd. Turn left or east on Brentwood, right on Charlotte and right on Olafson to Newport to complete this loop.

King's Park

Start	Path to the west of parking area
Distance	2.8 km
Parking	Parking Lot - King's Park

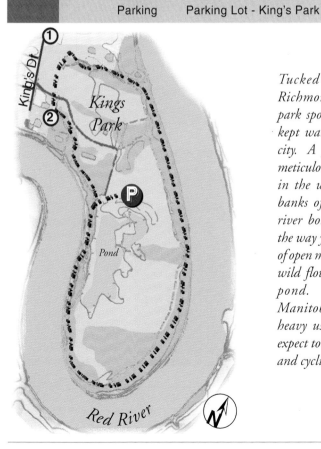

Tucked away in Fort Richmond, this riverside park sports one of the best kept walking paths in the city. A wide asphalt trail, meticulously cleared of snow in the winter, follows the banks of the Red through river bottom forest. Along the way you catch a glimpse of open meadows, waterfalls, wild flower gardens and a pond. University of Manitoba students make heavy use of this park, so expect to meet lots of joggers and cyclists.

The shallow lake complete with a small island and waterfowl nesting area, is the centre piece of the park. In summer, it is often pink with soft-stem Bulrushes that can grow eight feet high. The land excavated from the lake was used to build a hill at its north end and a rockery with three sets of waterfalls. River water is pumped in at the northwest corner of the park, and cascades down over the black granite bed of the waterfalls and into the lake. Two bridges connect to the island where a colourful Chinese pagoda, a gift of Winnipeg's Chinese Community, holds centre stage. Native chokecherry, buffalo berry, and jack pine flourish in the rockery, and there are also Sea buckthorn, creeping juniper, mugo pine and Nanking cherry.

King's Park was unique during the 1997 spring flood in that it was one of the few civic green spaces to be purposely flooded in order to save the surrounding neighbourhood. A dike was constructed just inside the

north border of the park by heavy construction equipment which removed earth and clay from the bermed area near the waterfall. After all usable clay was removed from the park, clean fill was trucked in. This resulted in a protective dike that was wider than 20 feet at the base and over 12 feet tall near the river. When the flood waters reached their peak, King's Park was flooded flush with the main entrance gate off King's Drive. It appeared as if the river had swallowed the park whole, with water depths ranging from one to over fifteen feet. The park is still recovering and some replanting is yet to be done. The new dike will be landscaped and incorporated into the park, and the pit where clay was "borrowed" will be developed into a feature. These changes will serve as a reminder of the great power of the Red River to reshape its surroundings.

The neighbourhood around King's Park wasn't developed until 1945.

1 *Side trip -* *Walk along the sidewalk of King's Drive north through the neighbourhood of Fort Richmond and to the University of Manitoba campus.*

One of its best known residents was Dr. E.J. Washington, who owned a good deal of property in the area. In fact the King's Park land was once called Washington Peninsula. There is a story fondly remembered, that when the doctor allowed a portion of this land to be worked by a market gardener, he insisted that a beautiful old elm tree be left unharmed.

2 That elm stands to this day, just a few feet off King's Drive on the right hand side of the park entrance roadway and is recognized as a heritage tree.

The south end of the park has a trellised sitting area from which you can view the arboretum and native wildflower and prairie grasses garden.

Start	Crescent Drive Park Picnic Shelter
Distance	3.2 km
Parking	Parking Lot - Crescent Drive Park

A walk on the woodland paths of this riverside city park and the quiet neighbourhood of Crescent Park.

Walk towards the river from the parking lot; then follow the dike path north past the boat launch to Crane Ave; turn up Crane Ave and follow it to Buxton Rd. Turn right off Crane onto a footpath between Buxton Rd and Sandra Bay.

The route through the park hugs a mile of river bank under tall shady trees, then follows the chain-link fence along the golf course . It meanders through the community of Crescent Park where many homes border on well treed green space and is recommended for a family outing. The circular trail ends at a very pleasant picnic area

and playground.

This area was a rural municipality of mostly unoccupied land with unbroken prairie as late as 1920's. Going back for centuries, this would have been prime sugar bush. Groves of Manitoba maples thrived in this crescent of rich alluvial soil

South Dr

Crane Ave

Sandra Bay

Pheasant

Holly Ave

South Dr

Crescent Drive Golf Course

Chain Link Fence

Crescent Drive Park

P

Crescent Dr

Red River

N

and their syrup provided an important source of food for early settlers.

The spring sugar making season was always a happy time, marking as it did the close of a hard prairie winter. Toward the end of March, when it was warm during the day but freezing at night, whole families would make their annual trip to the sugar camps. There was work for each member of the family. The men tapped the trees by cutting long slanting gashes in the trunk and driving in flat grooved wedges of wood. From these spigots, the sap, pale and colourless as water, dripped into pails hung below. Women and children gathered the sap and poured it into a big black cauldron over a hot fire. When boiled down sufficiently, it was poured into shallow dishes and left to harden, after which it was turned out in the form of a solid cake. Ordinarily it took 40 gallons of sap to produce one pound of sugar and a small camp might produce 25-30 lb. of sugar a season. Maple sugar was so important to early settlers that it was used as an item of trade.

Start	Wildwood St at Manchester Blvd
Distance	3.6 km
Parking	Manchester Blvd

This circle route winds through the woodsy neighbourhood of Wildwood Park and down a country lane that intersects the Wildewood Golf Course.

Begin on the pedestrian walkway that runs east and then south through the neighbourhood's central strip of parkland.

In 1946, Wildwood Park was the first residential 'garden suburb' on the Prairies. The development was intended to meet the housing shortage after

World War II, and the basic design was based on a highly celebrated development in Radburn, New Jersey. It's interesting that what began as a low cost housing experiment has turned into some very pricey and desirable real estate. Wildwood Park remains today the most unique housing development in the city.

All the homes in this 87 acre development face onto greenspace that is heavily treed and laced with pedestrian walkways. There are no streets running through the neighbourhood, just service lanes circling its periphery and behind the houses. The lanes form ten residential bays, identified alphabetically from A through J. Wildwood originally contained 281 houses with only five different floor plans available. The development proved so popular over the years, that most of these modest cottages have been transformed beyond recognition.

The park is filled with mature elms, ash and oak trees. Gardens are creatively landscaped. As you walk through the park there are many paths running east and west that you may wish to explore. If you do, it is recommended that you return to the designated route to continue on your way.

1 Once through the park and out on to South Drive, St. Johns Ravenscourt School is to your right. Through the trees of the Ravenscourt grounds, you can glimpse the rooftop of a Victorian mansion with a sad and romantic past. Colonel R.M. Thompson hired architect Cyril Chivers to design this house and had it built for his new bride. Before they could move in, he was called away to serve in World War I, where he died in battle. His distraught young widow refused to move into the house after that, and it remained empty for almost 20 years. With its aura of mystery, the mansion soon became a mini tourist attraction, and its private lane made a popular Sunday drive for Winnipeggers. The house is now used as a residence for St. Johns Ravenscourt students.

In winter, you are welcome to walk across the golf course greens and along the Red River dike.

Start	Path behind Riverview Health Centre
Distance	7.5 km
Parking	Baltimore Ave at Churchill Dr

This walk follows trails through a long narrow strip of green space called Churchill Park. It then loops through the quiet neighbourhood of Kingston Crescent and returns down the sidewalks of Riverview.

This entire area was the centre of Winnipeg's recreational life until the 2nd World War. The privately owned River Park carnival and exhibition grounds occupied all the land around Churchill Drive. Attractions included a miniature train, roller coaster, and zoo.

Before the turn of the century, people would ride a ferry across to Elm Park (now Kingston Crescent) where they would enjoy a midway featuring the latest in carnival amusements as well as walking paths through a forest of mature trees.

1 At the foot of Elm Park Bridge is an old fashioned ice cream stand that is something of a Winnipeg institution. Cross the picturesque old bridge to Kingston Crescent.

2 387 Kingston Crescent can claim the oldest American elm in the city and one of the most beautiful. That it is still standing is a tribute to its owner. Early in 1997, city workers detected Dutch Elm disease, and this 300 year old tree was tagged. The owner went to the work of having it injected with fungicide and it survived another season. With luck it will grace the s,treet for many years to come.

Riverview Health Centre

Baltimore Rd

Fisher St

Churchill Dr

Red River

Jubilee Ave

St Vital Bridge

Elm Park Foot Bridge

Kingston Cres

N

Start	Kingsway Ave
Distance	5.5 km
Parking	Kingsway at Wellington Cres

A stroll through an older neighbourhood with some of the most imposing homes in the city, our route also winds down the trendy Corydon strip and ends at Munson Park on the Assiniboine River.

Crescentwood was largely undeveloped until 1895 when a bridge was built over the Assiniboine at the site of the present Maryland Bridge. This coincided with the deterioration of the city's most affluent district near the present Fort Garry Hotel. In the days before zoning, conflicting land uses meant that a brewery might be located next door to a mansion. It was time to move!

Developer C.H. Enderton saw his opportunity and he was determined to make his new 'subdivision' of Crescentwood the most sought after address in the city. A caveat was placed on each lot, requiring the dwelling to be set back 60 feet from the front street line and have a value of at least $3500.00 - a tidy sum in those days. On Wellington Crescent the minimum figure was $6000. These restrictions ensured that single-family residential use would predominate, and Crescentwood has been a popular haven for the 'economically advantaged' ever since. Although there was a weakening of restrictions during the depression and World Wars, the spirit of the community was restored in 1952 when the Crescentwood Home Owners Association emerged and actively devoted themselves to maintaining the Enderton legacy of the single family neighbourhood.

Crescentwood contains some of the most impressive early 20th century homes in Winnipeg, if not in western Canada. A detailed historical walking tour of Crescentwood is available from the Manitoba Historical Society.

Corydon Avenue between Pembina and Stafford has a Mediterranean flavour with its cappuccino bars, Florentine light standards, and a fine assortment of restaurants. Nicknamed "Little Italy", this is one of the trendiest dining and shopping areas in the city.

Once past Munson Park's tyndall stone pillars and wrought iron fencing, you'll find woodlands that have been preserved in much of their original state. A.E. Munson, a Winnipeg lawyer, built Crescentwood Home here in the late 1880's. He retained the natural landscaping which was quite rare within the city at this time. In 1919, James Richardson purchased the property. His family lived here for 57 years until 1973, when they donated it to the city as a park. A plaque reads - "the existing trail through prairie scrub extending along the fence was originally created by natives and early pioneers, travelling from Upper Fort Garry to the West".

Start	Omand's Park
Distance	5.5 km
Parking	On Raglan Rd

This circle route crosses the Assiniboine twice and takes you through two very different neighbourhoods. Wellington Crescent has the highest concentration of grand mansions in the city and boasts a lovely centre boulevard complete with crushed stone walkway. The Wolseley area is generally viewed as Winnipeg's 'granola belt'. As of late, many young families have moved to the area, attracted by its strong sense of community, Laura Secord School, and handsome older houses.

Note: *During the summer months on Sundays and holidays, Wellington Crescent and Wolseley are limited to pedestrians and cyclists.*

②side trip *Instead of crossing the river at the railway bridge continue west across the railway tracks on a well maintained path along the river behind the old church yard to Wolseley West. St. James, the oldest wooden church left standing in Western Canada, was completed in 1853 at a cost of $1620. It still has services during summer months.* Note: A half dozen restaurants and a shopping mall are just one block up Tylehurst.

Entering Omand's Park off Raglan Rd, take note of 1339 Wolseley *(Pioneer Lodge)* , which was built by Frederick Salter around 1880. A skilled gardener, Salter owned the two lots east of Omands Creek and kept 26 greenhouses which supplied the C.P.R. trains from Montreal to Vancouver. Raglan Road was originally his private lane until the Wolseley

area was subdivided in 1910.

③ Not that long ago, Wellington Crescent was just an Indian trail following the curves of the river. There was no settlement until the mid 1880s, and locals referred to this part of town as 'the Bush'. In 1893 it was named for lawyer Arthur Wellington Ross who had purchased land in the area.

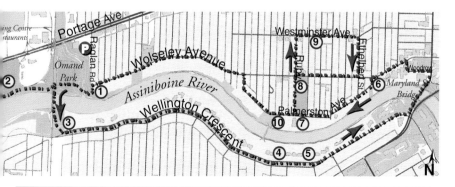

4 Most people do a double take at 1063 Wellington Cres. These half dozen lifesize sculptures by artist J. Seward Johnson add a dash of whimsy to the neighbourhood.

5 1015 Wellington Crescent (often referred to as the Eaton mansion) was designed by Arther Cubbidge in the mock Tudor style. Cubbidge was a British architect responsible for a number of massive houses in the city.

6 On Wolseley Ave between Chestnut and Canora, there are four distinctive brick houses on riverlot properties. The corner house (838 Wolseley) is one of only a handful of residences to have heritage building designation. Its back porches are particularly impressive and were built to signify the status of the owner to his Wellington Cres neighbours across the river.

Laura Secord School (960 **8** Wolseley) stands at the very heart of the neighbourhood. The architectural detail of the school was lovingly restored in 1980s, and the building stands as a symbol for the refurbishment taking place in many of the older homes in the area.

As evidenced by a proliferation of beautiful flowers on Wolseley area boulevards, gardening is a passion for many local residents. Robert A. Steen Community Club (980 Palmerston) **7** is home to

Morning Glories on Wolseley West

the Wolseley Garden Society, which organizes popular garden tours every summer. In front of the club, an elm tree has been planted to commemorate one of the city's most spectacular acts of civil disobedience. In 1957, twelve otherwise law abiding ladies defied city hall and won the right to save a landmark 100 year old elm tree from the ax.

1006 Palmerston is part of an original farm house built in the early 1870's (probably the oldest home in the area). The river farm lot originally extended two miles north across Portage to Notre Dame Avenue.

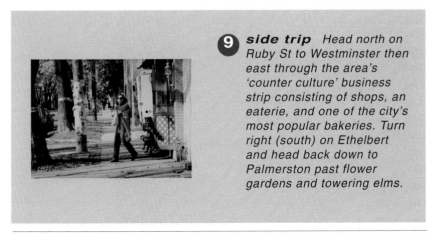

9 *side trip* Head north on Ruby St to Westminster then east through the area's 'counter culture' business strip consisting of shops, an eatery, and one of the city's most popular bakeries. Turn right (south) on Ethelbert and head back down to Palmerston past flower gardens and towering elms.

Bruce Park

Start	Assiniboine Park Footbridge
Distance	7 km
Parking	Parking lot by Duck Pond

Walking through this quiet neighbourhood of well kept homes and enormous gardens, you'll discover the wealth of green space these St. James residents enjoy.

From the duck pond, walk through the north edge of Assiniboine Park to a landmark footbridge on the Assiniboine River; cross over and then head west.

Bruce Park is named for two pioneer farmers who settled in this area. Today we can still enjoy the lilac bushes that James Bruce, an avid gardener, planted near what is now the west end of Deer Lodge Place.

A bronze plaque commemorates celebrated resident

LeMoine Fitzgerald (a member of Canada's famous "Group of Seven"), who lived at #30 Deer Lodge Place. Fitzgerald's painting of "Doc Snyders House" hangs in the National Gallery. Other works can be seen at the St. James Library and the Winnipeg Art Gallery.

This 13 acre park ② on the banks of Truro Creek is a showpiece with ancient trees, plantings of blue spruce and clump birch, wild roses, an ornamental footbridge, and rolling landscape.

3 A walk by the Bourkevale Community Club in the right season may reward you with a glimpse of the stately game of lawn bowling. The club has an active contingent of bowlers who put on a fine show on many a summer afternoon.

4 Bourkevale Avenue is named for John Bourke, one of the earliest farmers in the area and a celebrated buffalo hunter. Bourke was one of the many men who came out from the British Isles to work in the fur trade for the Hudson Bay Co. Like many of his co-workers, he fell in love with the place and decided to settle down on this part of the Assiniboine River.

6 A number of interesting shops and eateries have sprung up on Portage Ave across from the park footbridge. A coffee house, ice cream parlour and an antique and

5 *side trip* Follow paths through Bruce Park, cross creek bridge and exit on back lane near north end of park.
Proceed down lane to library; then turn right and follow informal path along back gardens of Douglas Park Rd . You'll be rewarded with a terrific glimpse of the massive lots and beautiful gardens on this street.

used book store provide an attractive destination for this walk.

WALK

21

Old Tuxedo

Start	Assiniboine Park Conservatory
Distance	4 km
Parking	Conservatory Parking Lot

This is an attractive walk that takes in rolling lawns, woodlands, formal flower gardens, a world famous sculpture garden, and the stately homes of Old Tuxedo. The loop begins and ends at the Assiniboine Park Conservatory.

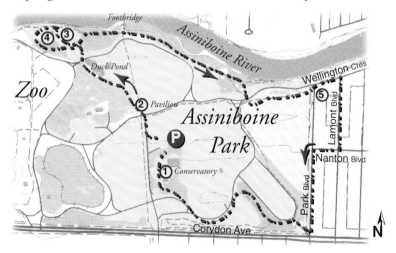

Assiniboine Park is what most of us grew up thinking of as a proper park - rolling lawns, wooded picnic sites, playgrounds, paved paths and plenty of trees. A zoo, conservatory, sculpture garden, and Tudor style pavilion complete the picture. As Winnipeg's largest park (393 acres), this is often referred to as 'City Park'.

The plan for Assiniboine Park, created in 1904, was based on the design of Frederick Law Olmsted - the father of landscape architecture in North America. The style is one that was used commonly throughout North America around the turn of the century and features curvilinear roadways, geometrical flower gardens, free form or serpentine ponds, and open meadows and lawns backed by borders of native plants. The curvilinear paths and roadways were meant to provide relief from the grid pattern of urban streets.

1 The Conservatory provides plant lovers with a year round lush oasis. It features a Palm house with tropical trees and exotic plants, and a continuous display of flowering and foliage plants in a garden setting.

2 The Pavillion was designed to suggest the English countryside and has been a city landmark for nearly 100 years. Work is under way to redevelop its interior as an art centre with a glass enclosed restaurant.

3 In summer, the English Garden is an explosion of colour with its formal flower beds of annuals and roses, and a lily pond surrounded by shade trees. At its east entrance, amidst the pool plantings is the 'Boy with the Boot' fountain statue. This statue is special to Winnipeggers. It was given to the city in 1897 by the Young People's Christian Endeavour Society and it used to stand in front of city hall. Then it disappeared and was listed as missing for 30 years. Mysteriously, it showed up by the duck pond in Assiniboine Park one day in the 1940's. The people at city hall were mystified but decided to install it right where it had been found.

4 Adjacent to the English gardens is the Leo Mol Sculpture Garden. Mol is a Winnipeg artist whose naturalistic sculptures are internationally renowned.

5 In 1913, the Town of Tuxedo was planned by a small group of men, as an exclusive and secluded development. To forestall any possibility of low or even medium-priced housing being built, a minimum value of $10,000 was imposed for each proposed dwelling. Each house had to be a minimum of 15 metres back from the street and each lot needed to measure at least 23 by 40 metres. These tight building regulations essentially dictated that each house have the look of a country estate, and in fact, many were patterned after grand Tudor or Georgian style English manor houses.

Leo Mol Sculpture Garden in Assiniboine Park

Start	Parking Lot at Grant and Chalfont
Distance	2.5 km one way

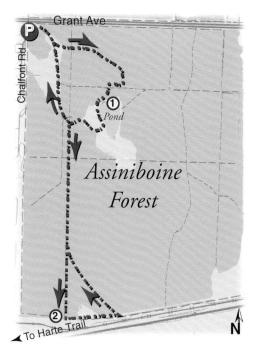

Grant Ave

Chalfont Rd

① *Pond*

Assiniboine Forest

②

To Harte Trail

N

Nowhere else within the boundaries of the city will a walker feel as surrounded by nature on this massive scale. This is a walk through an urban wilderness that offers the chance to enjoy nature in the heart of Winnipeg.

Assiniboine Forest is the largest urban forest park in Canada. It was established as a centennial project in 1974 and is maintained in its natural state, with the exception of the Eve Werier Memorial Pond.

This pond, named after Eve Werier, who devoted much of her time to wildlife preservation, is a man-made ecosystem constructed by Ducks Unlimited in the late 1970's. It supplies water for wild life and waterfowl, and with this water source, deer can be saved from crossing busy streets to reach the Assiniboine River. As well, the marsh is home to myriad wetland species - cattails, bulrushes and duckweed are most abundant. Early mornings or at dusk you may come upon deer drinking at water's edge or see a flock of ducks feeding on wetland plants.

Once you've left the asphalt path, heading south, you enter an aspen/oak forest consisting mainly of trembling aspen interspersed with oak. Underbrush includes dogwood, hazelnut, saskatoon, and chokecherry. This habitat is home to the white-tailed deer, the red squirrel, and the great horned owl.

Off the main trail you can see a number of paths which are very wet in spring. These paths are the road cuts made in 1920 in readiness for a housing development which fortunately never happened.

The route passes through many small prairie clearings that indicate a meadow ecosystem. These clearings contain a plant community very different from that in the aspen/oak forest and most of these prairie plant and animal species are becoming quite rare. Species include big bluestem grass, yellow lady slipper, bird foot violets and meadow blazingstar. Watch for kingbirds and meadowlarks.

At the south end of the park, our path abuts a footpath called the Harte Trail. This path runs west on an abandoned rail line to the perimeter highway and beyond. If you are truly adventurous you can follow it all the way to Beaudry Park.

Harte Trail Charleswood

Start	Ridgewood Ave & Haney St
Distance	4.5 km one way
Parking	Haney St

This former railway line is a 12 mile linear parkway running east/west from the south edge of Assiniboine Forest, through Charleswood, across the Perimeter Hwy and past Headingly to Beaudry Park.

Our walk picks up the trail at Haney St and Ridgewood Ave in Charleswood, where the path is most attractive. Over the years fruit bearing shrubs, Siberian elm and other native plants have grown up as shelter. This is a perfect local example of how a variety of natural growth takes over when land is left alone. The trail is regularly used for cycling and cross country skiing, as well as walking. Expect to share with dogs and cyclists.

The Harte Line was the first section built by the Grand Trunk Pacific Railway in western Canada and was in use from 1894 to 1972. It takes its name from a community further down the line, that no longer exists.

Along the path, a grove of spruce and another of cottonwood mark former farmsteads.

The path is intersected by half a dozen lightly travelled roads, and it is clear where the locals gain access, from numerous well worn footpaths meeting the trail. Housing developers continue to eye the land in this corridor, but Charleswood residents are wisely

protecting their wilderness strip.

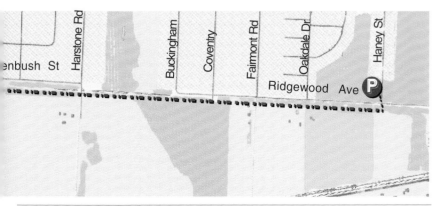

Start	Beaudry Park
Distance	10 km one way
Parking	Beaudry Park

For a real work-out, continue west along the Harte Trail past the Perimeter Highway, all the way to

Beaudry Park. This is the place to experience the prairie, right down to the classic sight of grain elevator silhouetted against the sky.

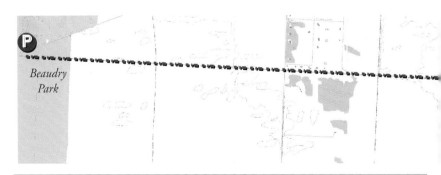

Beaudry Park

hawthorn. But the main attraction is classic prairie and that great panoramic view.

Drainage ditches have been cut through the rail bed at some of the mile roads, and one portion of the trail has been cultivated; so high boots may be needed when wet. The railway bridge over a small creek at Beaudry Park has been

This trail is now used mainly by cyclists, equestrians and snowmobilers, but it is so high, well packed and well drained, that it makes an excellent walking path. A great variety of wildlife finds protection here, and it is not uncommon to see deer grazing in the nearby fields or drinking from the ditches along the trail. Most of the rail line has remained undisturbed since abandonment in the 1970s and portions of this trail have been enhanced with a healthy growth of oak, aspen, Siberian elm and

removed. At this point use the secondary road. The trail ends very near the entrance to Beaudry Park

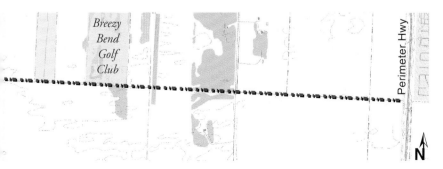

Breezy Bend Golf Club

Perimeter Hwy

N

WALK
25

Beaudry

Start	Beaudry Park parking lot or Dirt road south of PR241
Distance	North trail 7 km / South trail 5 km
Parking	Beaudry Park parking lot

This is a winding path through towering trees along the Assiniboine River. Beaudry Park boasts an exceptional forest of enormous trees, meadows with prairie flowers, 20 acres of pond and marsh and also remnants of tall grass prairie.

Beaudry is a natural park with a rare hardwood forest older than the city. The park is home to some of the largest cotton-woods in the province (14 ft. in circum-ference), as well as some 200 year old oaks, American elms that have survived Dutch Elm disease, large and magnificent willows, Manitoba maple and basswood, which are at the northern limit of their range. The towering trees are river bottom forest, so called because of periodic flooding of the encircling Assiniboine.

Wild grapes scale some of the trees to a height of 15 metres, growing on vines as thick as your arm. There is a diversity of terrain and a diversity of wildlife in the park. Some 95 species of song birds, as well as rabbits, squirrels, beaver, porcupine, coyotes, bears, wildcats, deer, elk and moose can be found.

The park was purchased by the province in 1974. It is 3.5 square miles in size and was named after a nearby railway siding.

Beaudry Park South

A road south of P.R. 241 leads to a trail which skirts the pond and upland nesting area. This 20

acre pond was designed to rejuvenate the marsh for waterfowl management and is maintained by Ducks Unlimited.

The wooded area to the west is full of saskatoons and chokecherrys.

As well, this is one of the last places in Canada with a remnant of tall grass prairie. This piece of our natural heritage has aroused global attention and is being protected by the Province. Here you can wander through giant blue stem and cord grass that grows taller than a man.

The cultivated fields are parkland but are rented out to a farmer - don't trespass. The trails will be muddy after a rain and in spring. Walking is best in fall.

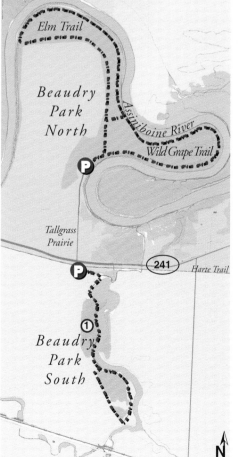

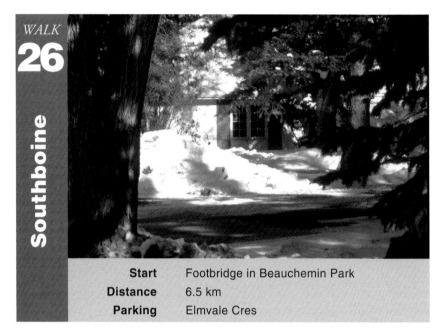

Southboine

Start	Footbridge in Beauchemin Park
Distance	6.5 km
Parking	Elmvale Cres

This trek through suburban greenspace is filled with historical significance.

From Elmvale Crescent, take the path across the Beaverdam Creek footbridge, through Beauchemin Park and out along Southboine Dr.

Beauchemin Park is named for Baptiste Beauchemin, one of the many Metis who were employed in the fur trade and later settled in Charleswood in the 1860's.

'The Passage' at the end of Berkley Ave is the site of an ancient ford on the Assiniboine and a designated cultural landmark. Shallow waters made this a choice location for bison herds to cross, and during the fur trade era, Native hunters guided the European traders to this ford.

Cuthbert Grant and his followers crossed here in 1816, trying to avoid the confrontation that resulted in the Battle of Seven Oaks, and Lord Selkirk's troops met Chief Peguis at The Passage in 1817 before recapturing Fort Douglas.

Caron Park has wide open meadows, dirt paths and bluffs of trees near the river that fit with the informal nature of this park. It is part of what was once four-mile strips of farmland running back from the Assiniboine to what is still

A path running north off Southboine between #6171 and #6191, leads to a greenspace named Kelly's Landing.

A store called Kelly's Landing was established near The Passage to capitalize on the flow of traffic. Today the Kelly's Landing site and the river bank property between it and Beauchemin Park are owned by the City of Winnipeg, which hopefully will develop and incorporate it in to the City Park system.

Follow Southboine west; cross a playground called Daly Gardens; then follow Barker Blvd to Musgrove St which takes you to the entrance of Caron Park.

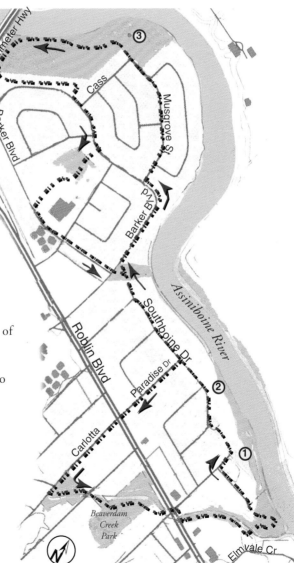

called Four Mile Road, south of Wilkes Ave. The first settlers were the Caron brothers in the 1880's, and the Caron farmhouse at the Musgrove entrance is the only original farmhouse left on the Assiniboine River. It gives a sense of this neighbourhood before the turn of the century.

The Carons built the first ferry to take their cheese across the Assiniboine to the Portage trail. In winter they would walk across the river ice to church. During spring break-up they needed to go all the way down to the Polo Park area to

cross the river, which meant an hour and a half journey to church each Sunday.

Exit park and turn left; follow Barker Blvd until you reach LaFleche Park. Cross the park and school grounds to Barker Blvd and turn left. Take Barker to Paradise Dr and turn right. Follow Paradise across Roblin to Beaverdam Creek Park. Follow the paths along the creek back across Roblin to your starting point. This linear parkway has no formal paths but the monkey trails are fun to explore.

'The Passage' - The Assiniboine River at the end of Berkley Ave

Start	Walking bridge at end of Woodbridge Rd
Distance	4.5 km one way
Parking	Woodbridge Rd

A long gentle walk through the neighbourhood of Woodhaven and the narrow parkway that follows Sturgeon Creek from the Assiniboine River to Saskatchewan Avenue.

Begin the walk near the junction of Sturgeon Creek and the Assiniboine River at Ashcrofts Point - a favorite fishing spot with the locals. A walking bridge over Sturgeon Creek leads to the community of Woodhaven and Woodhaven Park.

Woodhaven is a picturesque neighbourhood bounded by the Assiniboine River, Sturgeon Creek and the St Charles Country Club on the west. Residents enjoy a particularly fine vista of the broad Sturgeon Creek valley. The first houses built in

2 *Grant's Mill* - *A working replica of Grant's Mill was constructed in 1973 by an enterprising group of St. James-Assiniboia senior citizens. The mill is built from logs cut with a broad axe and held together with nails and wooden pegs. Since it was opened, the mill has survived the floods and become quite a tourist attraction .*

this area were summer homes, and the community has retained the air of a quieter and more relaxed time. There are no sidewalks and the older narrow roads wind and dip with the terrain.

 St Charles Country Club sets the standard for prestige. How many golf clubs can boast they've been played by the Prince of Wales? When first established in 1904, the club was so careful of its reputation that when the head of the household applied for membership, the entire family was screened. The price of membership was another challenge, with entrance fees at $100 on top of a $100 debenture and yearly membership at $25 for gentlemen, $10 for ladies, and $5 for clergymen.

Exit Woodhaven on an asphalt path under Portage Avenue which brings you out near Grant's Mill.

Grant's Mill is named for Cuthbert Grant who is best remembered as the leader of the Metis at the battle of Seven Oaks. Son of a Scottish father and a Cree mother, Grant was born in 1793 at a Northwest Co trading post where his father was the factor. He was sent to Scotland for his education and returned to work for the Northwest Co.

This is a replica of a mill constructed by Grant in the 1830s. It was the first of its kind to be built in the west and marks the first use of hydro power in this area. The mill was used for grinding flour and featured a huge water wheel. But Grant's enterprise encountered endless problems. The 230 foot dam that he constructed collapsed repeatedly, and eventually he was flooded out entirely and moved his operation to Grantown (now called St. Francis Xavier) and used a wind-driven mill.

From the mill, the path runs parallel to gently sloping grassy banks of the creek. While sections of the bank have been allowed to sprout some natural growth and a few areas have been planted to shrubs and perennials, for the most part, the parkway is open hay meadow. A change to allowing a more naturalized growth is apparent. Bridges and paths lead to the

This parkway was almost lost to development in the 1970's. Then, new municipal legislation was passed that required developers to set aside adequate space for parks and recreation and also preserve the natural features of the landscape when planning a new development. But legislation is often not enough when valuable land is at stake and in spite of the new agreement, the city was tempted to sell the land. Happily the citizens' cry could be heard - "Come hell or high water you can't have our creek" and their crusade saved the parkway from bulldozers.

suburban neighbourhoods of Crestview, Heritage Park and Sturgeon Creek. At Ness and Hamilton it is necessary to cross in traffic. By the time you reach Saskatchewan Avenue, open prairie is in view. This walk is best done in spring or fall, or early morning, as there is little shade from the sun on a hot summer day.

Living Prairie

Start	Living Prairie Museum
Distance	2 km
Parking	Living Prairie Museum at 2795 Ness Ave

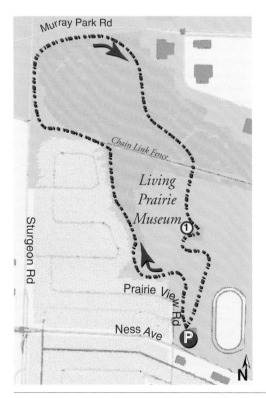

This short circle walk features one of the last remaining stands of tallgrass prairie in Manitoba. Trails through the tallgrass fields lead to monkey trails through a wooded area that backs onto quiet suburban Assiniboia and then back to the prairie.

The Living Prairie Museum nature park is a 30 acre tallgrass prairie preserve containing hundreds of prairie plants and a great assortment of prairie wildlife.

Close to 20,000 years ago, a great glacier covered this province moving soil and sediment from the north and dumping it in the south. When the glacier melted, it left a lake - Lake Agassiz. When most of the lake either evaporated or drained, it left behind a rich bed of soil in which the prairie was born. The heavy impervious soil of the tallgrass prairie locality and the flatness of the land result in poor drainage. The dominant grasses are those species such as big bluestem and Indian grass which grow well in moist areas. Other plants common in the tallgrass prairie are the prairie crocus, three flowered avens, goldenrod, narrow-leaved sunflower, and meadow blazingstar.

Tallgrass prairie once occupied 1.5 million acres in Manitoba alone. Today, less than one percent remains, making tallgrass prairie the most endangered habitat in North America. Winnipeg is fortunate to have one of the highest grades of tall grass prairie left in Manitoba.

A sea of waving grass greeted the first explorers to the Winnipeg region. Soon after, the creak of ox carts became a common sound as hundreds of settlers flowed to the area in search of a better life. Their first homes were often built of the sod they ploughed to plant their crops. The plough exposed rich soils in which crops flourished. Unfortunately the plough resulted in the death of much of the tallgrass prairie and the wildlife it supported. With the merchants came improved technology and modern agriculture. The result was the ploughing of 99% of tallgrass prairie into the pages of history. The tallgrass, wild flowers, bison, wolf and plains grizzly bear were not the only victims of development. An entire way of life for the Swampy Cree and Ojibway peoples was also pushed aside.

1 This shelterbelt area is the site of the Andrew McDermot homestead. In 1812, McDermot migrated to the Red River Valley with Lord Selkirk. His lot 12, an 840 acre tract fronting on the Assiniboine River, extended two miles north across the prairie.

Little Mountain

Start	Parking lot on Farmers Rd
Distance	2 km

This park has an interesting history. More than 100 years ago, it was home to a village named Mount Royal and a stone crushing operation

which was the first limestone quarry of the city of Winnipeg. At peak production, 164 families lived here and worked in the quarry. The village had two blacksmith shops, a pool hall, and even a bootlegger. But by 1905 it became too costly to mine in this location.

The crusher was dismantled and moved by horse-drawn sled to the present day quarry at Stony Mountain.

Little Mountain is a natural park with a large section of aspen forest. Bur oak, saskatoon, wild plum and chokecherry, as well as dogbane and raspberry, make a dense undergrowth in this edge environment which is home to the red fox.

Our path takes you

Little Mountain Park is a height of land on a limestone ridge. Our path runs through 80 acres of heavy woodland and around an old quarry. From a rock outcropping at the south end of the park, the whole skyline of Winnipeg is clearly visible ten miles in the distance.

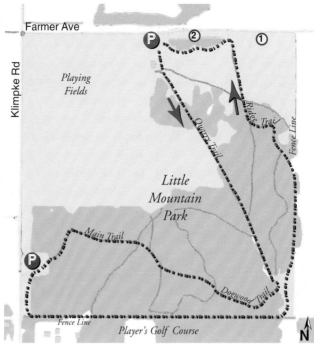

Farmer Ave

Klimpke Rd

Playing Fields

Little Mountain Park

Quarry Trail

Ridge Trail

Fence Line

Main Trail

Dogwood Trail

Fence Line

Player's Golf Course

N

through authentic prairie. Crocuses can be seen almost as soon as the snow melts and are succeeded by a continuous bloom of wildflowers throughout the summer. Three flowered Avens, Puccoon, Gallardia and Prairie lilies are some of the blossoms that flourish in this grass parkland.

1 This beautifully shaped Cottonwood is the last remaining planted tree of the lost village of Mount Royal.

2 One of the nicest features of this park is the old quarry pits - now a scenic pond and picnic site. Paths take you down to the shoreline of large jagged rocks where limestone walls tower up around you. This is a watering hole for mammals and migratory birds and supports a growth of true water plants.

LaBarrier Park

Start	Parking Lot - LaBarrier Park
Distance	West Trail 2.6 km / East Trail 4.8 km

Riverbank trails through acres of grassland and lowland forest on the banks of the LaSalle.

Waverly Street leads directly to La Barrier Park which is 3/4 of a mile south of the perimeter highway. There's a sharp dip in the road before the park entrance at the LaSalle River bed. It's also marked by a dam across the river, where you can spot fishermen trying their luck.

The park is named for the barrier erected by Louis Riel's followers in 1869. Their act effectively prevented the entry of arms and an unauthorized governor, sent by Ottawa, into the Red River settlement. It was a watershed event in the Metis battle for self-

government and a cross standing in St Norbert marks the historic site.

LaBarrier offers an enormous riverbank trail system on the river's wooded banks. The lowland forest rolls gently on either side with graceful groves of ash, elm and large stands of oak. Some of the land consists of original farm river lots, with the woods preserved intact.

This linear river parkway is preserving a unique landscape. The southwest corner of the park is left untended to illustrate the natural

West trail - Cross rolling clipped grassland to the river. A wooden spanned bridge leads to several kilometres of trail through heavy woods far from the nearest road. Take a circle route through the woods and along the edge of cultivated fields. In late spring you may see schools of catfish in the river.

Waverly St

LaSalle River

East Trail

East trail - Follow a rough and uneven path along the winding river and return by heading south through the grasslands of Boy Scouts' Camp Amisk.

Foot Bridge

West Trail

La Barriere Park

N

state of river forest. The park is also a site for testing the effectiveness of reseeding of native vegetation.

Picnic areas have been mostly cleared of underbrush and given an open and natural setting. The scrub oak trees that dot the upper area are gradually being replaced with elm and ash. Although the city has done some landscaping it is always with the idea of keeping this area a natural beauty spot.

Residents of St. Norbert have drawn up long-range plans for the city to acquire sufficient riverbank access so that a trail eight kilometres long would link La Barrier to the St. Norbert Community Centre on the Red River.

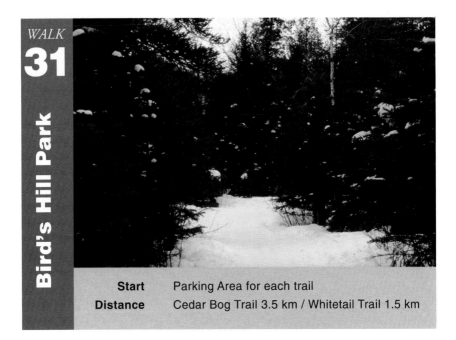

Start	Parking Area for each trail
Distance	Cedar Bog Trail 3.5 km / Whitetail Trail 1.5 km

Good paths for walking in the winter are at a premium in our city. We've selected two of the best in Bird's Hill Park. They're both quite sheltered and nice snow-packed.

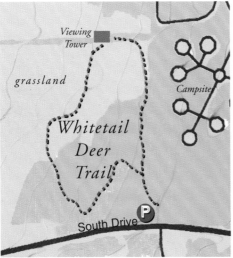

The White-tailed Deer Trail meanders through aspen groves and across large meadows. Here you will have opportunity to see deer in their natural habitat. Just after sunset or early in the day you may spot a white tailed deer feeding along the edge of a clearing. If alarmed, the deer will snort and bound away with white tail raised and waving side to side, warning other deer of your presence. A viewing tower is located midway along the trail.

Parts of Birds Hill have an elevation as much as 150 feet above that in Winnipeg. In the great floods of 1826 and 1852, settlers and wildlife found refuge here. Families camped for weeks with their livestock and all the possessions they could carry.

The unique Birds Hill landscape is really a series of eskers or massive sand and gravel deposits left behind by melted glaciers. As well, the land was sculpted by Lake Agassiz as it drained. Boulders were dropped by melting icebergs 10,000 years ago and as the lake level lowered, Birds Hill became an island. Whenever the lake's level remained constant for several decades, gravelly beaches were formed on the island's shore.

Today, these beach ridges are evident along the Cedar Bog Trail

The Cedar Bog Trail winds through stands of aspen and oak interspersed with patches of lush grassland before it descends gently into a unique cedar bog. Here the tall eastern white cedars create a canopy which blocks sunlight and creates mysterious shadows. In winter, brilliant yellow evening grosbeak , black capped chickadees and redpols frequent bird feeders set along the trail.

Winter Walk Only

WALK 32

Seine River Parkway

Start	St Boniface Golf Club Parking Lot at 100 Youville
Distance	6 km

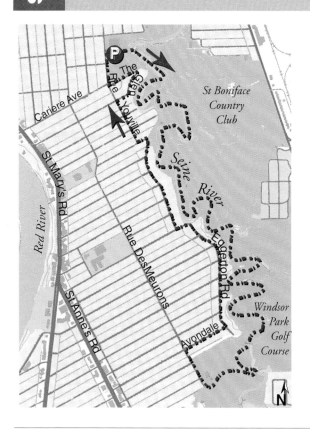

The first section of this route is on the ice covered Seine River which has a sheltered well-trodden path in winter. The return route is through the quiet neighbourhood of Glenwood.

Our route begins at the club house of the privately owned St. Boniface Country Club whose members generously allow walkers access in the winter. Walk down to the river bed and proceed south or to the right. The Seine River takes the typical meandering course of most rivers on the flat prairie, and its frozen bed offers a unique place to walk mid winter. When the sun is shining, the light slanting through branches on the well treed banks creates an exquisite scene. On the west bank is the neighbourhood of Glenwood with some of the nicest back yards in Winnipeg. The locals make heavy use of the river as a pathway and for skating and skiing.

For many years the Seine was used as a garbage dump and its potential ignored, but in 1990 a group of concerned citizens formed the Save Our Seine (S.O.S.). The organization was born out of concern for the plight of this river which flowed past many of their back yards. The group got together volunteer cleanup crews every Thanksgiving and hauled barge loads of shopping carts, old tires and sunken lumber out of the water. Each year more volunteers showed up for the annual blitz. In 1994 even the Lieutenant Governor Yvon Dumont built a raft, rolled up his jean cuffs, and took to the water to help in the cleanup. S.O.S. is now working toward restoration of the river bottom forest running along its banks and looking at environmentally friendly ways to make the river usable for recreation.

The riverbanks are a unique habitat. Large Manitoba maple, green and black ash, American elm, plains cottonwood, basswood and sandbar willow stand with their undergrowth of ostrich ferns and wood nettle. The uplands edges of the flood plains forest merge with bur oak, big bluestem, high bush cranberry, American hazelnut, saskatoon, snowberry, wild rose and wild red raspberry.

WALK
33

St Norbert LaSalle

Start	Trappist Monastery Park
Distance	3.2 km one way

We have snowmobilers to thank for this snow-packed pathway on the frozen La Salle River. Begin at Trappist Monastery Historical Park and follow the river to St. Norbert Provincial Heritage Park on the Red.

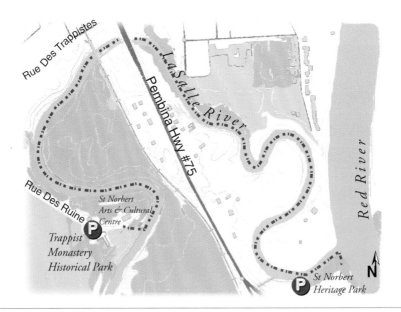

The LaSalle is a lovely winding river bordered by thick groves of trees. Spots of evergreen and the red bark of dogwood add welcome colour to a world of white. Here and there, matted grass hangs from branches high above as evidence of the height of the river during spring flood.

Trappists decided to move to more remote southwestern Manitoba. Subsequently, the citizens of St. Norbert worked to preserve this site, and even though the vacant chapel and residential wing were gutted by fire in 1983, the restored ruins became a provincial heritage park in 1987.

Remains of the tyndall stone chapel and monastery - 'the Ruins', date back to 1892 when the Trappist Order of Monks became established here. At one time, they ran a thriving agricultural operation with 37 priests busily engaged in tending bees and milking cows. They were completely cut off from the rest of the world, and the isolation of the place was vitally important to these monks. Over time this seclusion became threatened by encroaching development, and in 1978 the

St Norbert Arts and Cultural Centre now occupies the four storey Guest House built by the Trappists in 1912. This eye-catching building with its dormer windows, 12 foot ceilings, and gleaming hardwood floors, has been declared a provincial heritage site.

The city has recently acquired, as park space, 121 acres of forest on the south bank of the river. For years, this natural wooded area has been a favourite of local residents who like to ski and ride horses through the park. Over time, the city plans to build an 8 km nature walk from the forks of the Red and Seine rivers all the way to LaBarrier Park.

St. Norbert Heritage Park gives us a glimpse of how people lived here 125 years ago. There are five houses of early Metis and French Canadians from the time of the Red River Resistance. As you climb up and reach the high bank where the LaSalle meets the Red, look north for a memorable view of the river. The Park was designed to illustrate how a natural landscape, once used for hunting, fishing and camping by Native peoples, evolved into a French-speaking Metis settlement, then a French agricultural community of the pre-World War I period.

Another development planned for the park is the reconstruction of an early Indian camp site The region near the mouth of the LaSalle River may have been occupied by human beings as early as 6000 B.C. An ancient Palaeo Indian spearhead was found near a small stream that flows into the LaSalle at St. Norbert. This artifact, made of a type of stone that occurs naturally in the Canadian Shield, probably represents the seasonal movement of hunters from the forest to the grassland to hunt buffalo.

The Trans Canada Trail in Winnipeg

The Trans Canada Trail will be the longest walking trail in the world and by the year 2000, it will wind its way through every Province and Territory. It will be a shared-use trail for walkers, cyclists, cross country skiers, and in some cases, horseback riders, and snowmobilers.

The first portion of the Trans Canada Trail to be designated in Manitoba, is a route here in Winnipeg that stretches from the Forks to Kildonan Park. This overlaps two of our walks - Scotia Street and Point Douglas - Walks #4 & #5. It is the Manitoba Recreational Trail Association, a charitable organization of which we are members, which is hard at work planning and constructing the TRANS CANADA TRAIL in our province. MRTA is identifying, mapping, and building a corridor of 'linear parks' that connect communities, history and nature for all of us to enjoy.

To get involved in Manitoba Recreational Trail activities, contact the MRTA office at:

Manitoba Recreation Trail Association
204 - 825 Sherbrook St
Winnipeg, Manitoba
R3A 1M5

Information on national progress of the Trans Canada Trail can be found at the TCT Website: **www.tctrail.ca**

Winnipeg Transit Service to Trail Head

#	Walk	Route	Bus Stop
1	Assiniboine Parkway	17 McGregor	Wolseley Ave at Misericordia Hospital
2	Osborne Village	16 Osborne Selkirk	Osborne St & Broadway Ave
3	Forks Circle	38 Salter	Forks Market Rd
4	Point Douglas	38 Salter	Forks Market Rd
5	Scotia Street	18 North Main-Corydon	Armstrong St at Kildonan Park
6	Bunn's Creek	11 Kildonan-Portage	Knowles Ave
7	Kildonan Drive	11 Kildonan-Portage	Sutton Ave
8	Old St Boniface	10 St Boniface-Wolseley	St Joseph N
9	Central St Boniface	10 St Boniface-Wolseley	DesMeurons & Provencher
10	Niakwa Park	57 Southdale	Archibald at Cottonwood
11	St Vital	76	Kilmarnock
12	Normand Park	14 & 54 St Mary's Rd	Normand Park Dr
13	Maple Grove	14 & 54 St Mary's Rd	end of line
14	Kings Park	62 & 72 Richmond	Silverstone
15	Crescent Drive	94	Crane at South Dr
16	Wildwood	94	Oakenwald
17	Riverview	95	Riverview Health Centre
18	Crescentwood	68 Crescent	Wellington Cres at Hugo
19	Wolseley-Wellington Cres	21 Portage Express	Valour Rd
20	Bruce Park	21 Portage Express	Overdale at Portage Ave
21	Old Tuxedo	67 Charleswood Express	Corydon & Shaftesbury
22	Assiniboine Forest	65 Grant or 66 Grant Express	Chalfont & Grant
23	Harte Trail Charleswood	65 Grant or 66 Grant Express	Grant at Haney
24	Harte Trail Headingly	65 Grant or 66 Grant Express	End of line
25	Beaudry	no bus service	
26	Southboine	67, 79 Charleswood Express	Roblin Blvd at Berkley
27	Sturgeon Creek Parkway	21 Portage Express	Portage Ave at Thompson Dr
28	Living Prairie	24 Ness Express	PrairieView Rd
29	Little Mountain Park	no bus service	
30	LaBarrier	no bus service	
31	Bird's Hill Park	no bus service	
32	Seine River Parkway	14 Ellice - St Mary	Carriere
33	St Norbert LaSalle	62 Richmond	Des Trappistes

Selected Bibliography

Artbise, Alan. *Winnipeg in maps 1816-1872.* National Map Collection, Ottawa, 1974

_____ *Winnipeg; an illustrated history.* Lorimer, Ottawa, 1977

_____ *Winnipeg: a social history of urban growth.* McGill Queens Univ. Press, Montreal, 1974

Bumstead, J.M. *The Red River Rebellion.* Watson & Dwyer, Winnipeg, 1996

Crescentwood: Winnipeg's finest community; a walking tour. Manitoba Historical Society, Winnipeg.

Doolan, Maureen. *Downtown Winnipeg's Historic Sites & Monuments.* City of Winnipeg; City Centre Fort Rouge Community, Winnipeg, 1979

Fort Rouge Neighbourhood Walking Tour. City of Winnipeg, Winnipeg, 1994

Gibbons, Lillian. *Stories Houses Tell.* Hyperion, Winnipeg, 1978

Guinn, Rodger. *The Red-Assiniboine Junction: a land use and structural history 1770-1980.* Parks Canada, Ottawa, 1980

Healy, William. *Women of the Red River.* Peguis, Winnipeg, 1923

Henderson, Anne M. *Kildonan on the Red.* Winnipeg Lord Selkirk Assoc., Winnipeg, 1981

Macdonald, Catherine. *A City at Leisure.* City of Winnipeg, Winnipeg, 1995

MacLeod, Margaret. *Cuthbert Grant of Grantown.* McClelland, Toronto, 1974

Manitoba 125: a history (Vol 1). Great Plains Publications, Winnipeg, 1994

Manitoba 125 a history (Vol 2). Great Plains Publications, Winnipeg, 1994

Manitoba 125 a history (Vol 3). Great Plains Publications, Winnipeg, 1994

Manitoba Forestry Assoc. *Heritage Trees of Manitoba.* Canadian Forestry Service, Ottawa, 1987

Manitoba Heritage Site designation and heritage building Grants. Annual report 1980-1992. Manitoba Culture, Heritage & Citizenship, Historic Resources, Winnipeg.

Marr, Ruth. *Manitoba: Walking & Hiking guide.* Fifth House, Saskatoon, 1990

McFee, Janice. *Famous Manitoba Metis.* Manitoba Metis Federation Press, Winnipeg, 1974

Minnesota Historical Society. *The Red River Trails; oxcarts routes between St. Paul and the Selkirk Settlement 1820-1870.* Minnesota Historical Soc.   St. Paul, 1979

Mitchell, Alan. *The Pocket Guide to Trees of North America.* Prospero, London, 1998

Muddy Waters: an interpretive Guide to Winnipeg's Rivers. City of Winnipeg, Winnipeg, 1982

Nicholson, Karen. *The Passage.* (unpublished report for Dept. of Culture & Heritage), 1989

On the East of the River - a history of the East Kildonan Transcona community. City of Winnipeg, Winnipeg

Peterson, Murray. *Winnipeg Landmarks Vol 1.* Watson Dwyer, Winnipeg, 1995

Peterson, Murray. *Winnipeg Landmarks Vol 2.* Watson Dwyer, Winnipeg, 1998

Peterson, Roger. *Peterson"s first guide to birds of North America.* Houghton, New York, 1986

Porth, Laural. *Strong Currents: a history of Sturgeon Creek.* Sturgeon Creek Assoc., Winnipeg, 1995

Reimer, Mavis. *Wildwood Park through the years.* Wildwood History Book, Winnipeg, 1989

Riel House National Historic Park; interpretive manual. Parks Canada, Ottawa, 1988

Rostecki, Randy R. *Crescentwood a history.* Crescentwood Homeowners Assoc., Winnipeg, 1993

Russenholt, E.S. *The Heart of the Continent*. MacFarlane, Winnipeg, 1968

Schmidt, Anita A. *On the banks of the Assiniboine: a history of the parish of St. James*. City of Winnipeg, Winnipeg, 1975

Seine River Parkway. City of Winnipeg, Winnipeg, 1995

Self Guide to Downtown Winnipeg's Historic Sites & Monuments. City of Winnipeg, Winnipeg

Silver, Alfred. *Red River Story*. Ballatine, New York, 1988

St. Boniface. Manitoba Culture, Heritage & Recreation, Historic Resources Branch, Winnipeg, 1994

St. Charles Country Club 1905-1965. s.n., Winnipeg, 1966

St. Norbert Heritage Park, Manitoba. Manitoba. Historic Resources Branch, Winnipeg, 1983

Sternberg, Guy. *Landscaping with Native Trees*. Chapters, Shelburne, 1995

Tellier, Corrine. *Revisiting St. Norbert: a south Winnipeg Community*. Fort Garry Historical Society, Winnipeg, 1996

The Red River Rising: the Flood of the Century. Winnipeg Free Press, Winnipeg, 1997

Thompson, William. *Winnipeg Architecture*. Winnipeg: Queeston House,1975

Tuxedo; a history and walking tour. Winnipeg: Manitoba Historical Society, 1991

Vance, Fenton R. *Wildflowers across the Prairies* . Greystone Books, Vancouver,1992

Walking in Wolseley. Manitoba Historical Society, Winnipeg.

Wells, Eric. *Winnipeg: where the new west begins: an illustrated history*. Burlington: Windsor Publications,1982

'Where it all began" the history of the Lord Selkirk-West Kildonan Community. City of Winnipeg, Winnipeg,1982

Winnipeg centennial souvenir book, Provost Publishing,   Winnipeg,1974

Winnipeg Free Press (Vertical files of Winnipeg Public Library & scrap books of the Legislative Library)

Winnipeg Real Estate News (Vertical file clippings from Winnipeg Public Libraries)

Winnipeg Tribune (Clippings- vertical files of Winnipeg Public Library & verital file clippings & scrap books of Legislative library)

And a large variety of pamphlets about Winnipeg published by various levels of government, local organizations and institutions